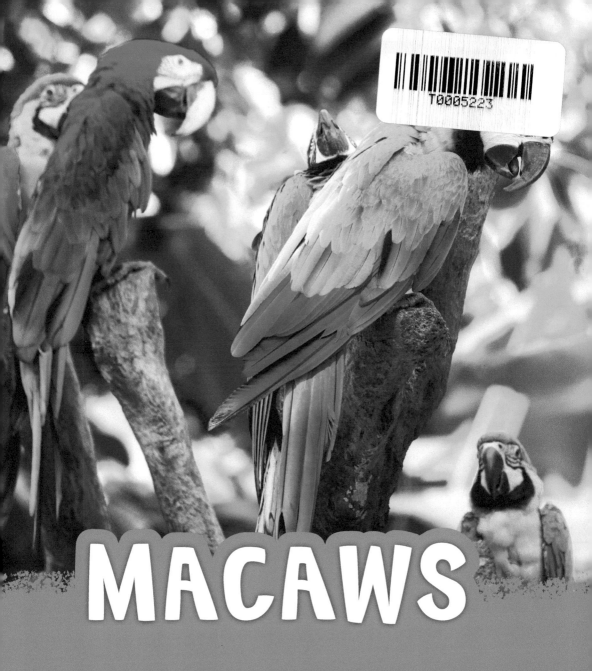

MACAWS

by Jaclyn Jaycox

PEBBLE
a capstone imprint

Pebble Explore is published by Pebble, an imprint of Capstone.
1710 Roe Crest Drive
North Mankato, Minnesota 56003
www.capstonepub.com

Library of Congress Cataloging-in-Publication Data
Names: Jaycox, Jaclyn, 1983- author.
Title: Macaws / by Jaclyn Jaycox.
Description: North Mankato, Minnesota : Pebble, [2021] | Series: Animals | Includes bibliographical references and index. | Audience: Ages 6-8 | Audience: Grades K-1 | Summary: "Macaws are among the most colorful members of the parrot family. These smart birds live in the rain forest. They use their bony tongues to crack into nuts and seeds. Find out more about these fancy fliers!" — Provided by publisher.
Identifiers: LCCN 2020044494 (print) | LCCN 2020044495 (ebook) | ISBN 9781977131973 (hardcover) | ISBN 9781977132994 (paperback) | ISBN 9781977154583 (pdf) | ISBN 9781977156259 (kindle edition)
Subjects: LCSH: Macaws—Juvenile literature.
Classification: LCC QL696.P7 J39 2021 (print) | LCC QL696.P7 (ebook) | DDC 598.7/1—dc23
LC record available at https://lccn.loc.gov/2020044494
LC ebook record available at https://lccn.loc.gov/202004449

Image Credits
Capstone Press, 6; Shutterstock: Charles Bergman, 21, Eric Isselee, 23, GTW, 22, Ian Duffield, 12, 25, Independent birds, 7, Jiri Hrebicek, 8, Jo Reason, 26, JueWorn, 27, KAMONRAT, 17, khonlangklong, 13, Niels van der Horst, 14, Ondrej Prosicky, 11, 28, Passakorn Umpornmaha, 18, Stanislav Duben, Cover, Super Prin, 10, terekhov igor, 1, 5

Editorial Credits
Editor: Hank Musolf; Designer: Dina Her; Media Researcher: Morgan Walters; Production Specialist: Tori Abraham

Table of Contents

Words in **bold** are in the glossary.

Amazing Macaws

The sun rises in the rain forest. Animals chatter away. You hear a trickling stream. You see a rainbow through the leaves above. Wait—that's not a rainbow. It's a macaw!

These bright, colorful animals are a type of bird. They are the largest birds in the parrot family. There are 18 kinds of macaws.

Where in the World

Macaws are found in Central and South America. They live in warm areas. They can be found between southern Mexico and northern Argentina.

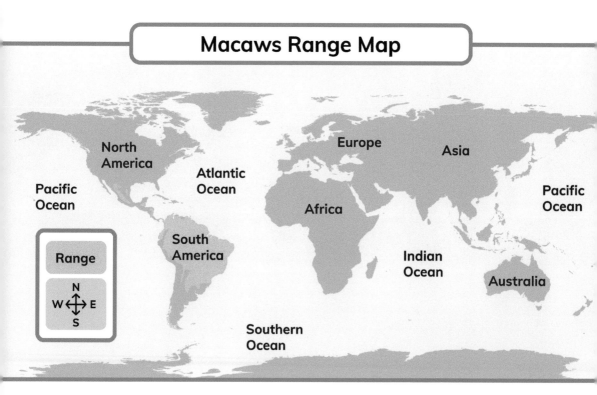

Macaws Range Map

North America

Europe

Asia

Atlantic Ocean

Pacific Ocean

Africa

Pacific Ocean

Range

South America

Indian Ocean

N
W ⟷ E
S

Australia

Southern Ocean

Most of these birds live in **tropical** rain forests. They can be found in woodlands and flat, grassy areas too.

Macaws live in trees. They spend their nights under the forest **canopy**. They sleep on branches.

During the day, they fly to their feeding grounds. Sometimes they travel up to 15 miles (24 kilometers) away. They find groups of trees full of fruit to eat. They spend all day there. Then they fly back home before sunset.

Colorful Chatterboxes

Macaws are known for their bright colors. They have red, yellow, blue, and green feathers. They have long tails.

It might seem like their colors make them stand out. But bright feathers help keep them hidden. The colors blend in with bright fruits, flowers, and green leaves.

hyacinth macaw

Macaws are big birds. Their bones are very light. This makes it easier for macaws to fly. They weigh between 2 and 4 pounds (0.9 and 1.8 kilograms).

The largest is the hyacinth macaw. It grows up to 3.5 feet (1 meter) long. Its wingspan is about 5 feet (1.5 m) wide.

The smallest is the Hahn's macaw. It is about 12 inches (30 centimeters) long. That's shorter than a bowling pin! It weighs less than 6 ounces (170 grams).

Hahn's macaw

Macaws fly easily through the trees. They are thin and long. Some macaws can fly up to 40 miles (64 km) per hour. When they land, they use their wings to slow down. Their long toes are perfect for gripping tree branches.

Macaws are smart and loud! They squawk and screech to talk to other birds. They can also copy sounds. Some are kept as pets. They can even learn to talk.

On the Menu

Macaws eat lots of different foods. They eat fruit, flowers, leaves, nuts, and seeds. They eat bugs, and snails too.

Macaws have very strong **beaks**. They can break through the shells of nuts and seeds. Some can even crack coconut shells! These birds have dry, hard tongues. They use them to dig into the fruits they eat.

Macaws eat clay along riverbanks too. People are not sure why they do this. The clay has **minerals** in it. It is good for the birds. It may also help with **digestion**.

Some of the seeds and fruits macaws eat are poisonous. Scientists think the clay helps the birds so they don't get sick.

Life of a Macaw

Macaws live in groups called flocks. Some can have as many as 30 birds. The birds are safer living in flocks. There are many birds to watch for **predators**. If there is danger, they all take off flying. Doing this confuses the predator. It gives the birds time to get away.

Macaws **mate** for life. The pairs clean each other's feathers and share food. They sit together on tree branches. The birds are never far away from each other. They even fly close together. Their wings almost touch!

Macaws make nests in **hollow** trees.
They make nests on the sides of cliffs.

They lay eggs once a year. The female lays between one and four eggs. She keeps them warm. The male brings food back for her. After three to four weeks, the eggs hatch.

Macaws are born with few feathers. Their eyes stay closed for two to three weeks. Both parents help take care of the babies.

Babies grow their feathers at about 10 weeks old. After three months, they start to learn to fly. Soon they go with their parents to find food. They stay together for about one year. Then the young fly off on their own.

Macaws live long lives. Most live about 50 years. Some can live much longer. One macaw is believed to be more than 110 years old!

Dangers to Macaws

Macaws have some predators.
Large snakes and eagles attack them.
Jaguars and monkeys do too.

Humans are also a danger to macaws. It is against the law to catch them. But some people still do it. They sell them as pets.

Humans are also cutting down rain forests. These birds are losing their homes.

Almost all types of macaws are in danger of dying out. But some people are trying to save them. They are working to protect the land they live on. They are planting more trees.

Macaws are taken away from people who catch them. They are given to groups that help the birds. These groups work hard to get them back to the wild.

Fast Facts

Name: macaw

Habitat: tropical rain forests, woodlands, flat, grassy areas

Where in the World: Central and South America

Food: fruit, flowers, nuts, seeds, leaves, bugs, and snails

Predators: eagles, large snakes, jaguars, monkeys, humans

Life Span: 50 years

Glossary

beak (BEEK)—the hard front part of the mouth of birds

canopy (KAN-uh-pee)—the treetops in a forest

digestion (dye-JESS-chuhn)—the process a body uses to turn food into energy

hollow (HOL-oh)—empty on the inside

mate (MATE)—to join with another to produce young

mineral (MIN-ur-uhl)—a material found in nature that is not an animal or a plant

predator (PRED-uh-tur)—an animal that hunts other animals for food

tropical (TRAH-pi-kuhl)—hot and wet; places near the equator are tropical

Read More

Huddleston, Emma. *Looking into the Rain Forest.* Mankato, MN: The Child's World, 2020.

Schuh, Mari C. *The Supersmart Parrot.* Minneapolis: Lerner Publications, 2018.

Statts, Leo. *Parrots.* Minneapolis: Abdo Zoom, 2018.

Internet Sites

Ducksters—Blue and Yellow Macaw
ducksters.com/animals/blue_and_yellow_macaw.php

Easy Science for Kids—Scarlet Macaw
easyscienceforkids.com/scarlet-macaw/

Kiddle—Macaw Facts for Kids
kids.kiddle.co/Macaw

Index